John Kemp

The Gospel Adapted to the State and Circumstances of Man

a sermon peached before the Society in Scotland for Propagating Christian Knowledge

John Kemp

The Gospel Adapted to the State and Circumstances of Man
a sermon peached before the Society in Scotland for Propagating Christian Knowledge

ISBN/EAN: 9783337160654

Printed in Europe, USA, Canada, Australia, Japan

Cover: Foto ©Lupo / pixelio.de

More available books at **www.hansebooks.com**

THE GOSPEL ADAPTED TO THE STATE AND CIRCUMSTANCES OF MAN.

A SERMON

PREACHED BEFORE

THE SOCIETY IN SCOTLAND
FOR PROPAGATING CHRISTIAN KNOWLEDGE;

AT THEIR ANNIVERSARY MEETING

IN THE HIGH CHURCH OF EDINBURGH,

Thursday, June 5. 1788.

BY THE REV. JOHN KEMP,

ONE OF THE MINISTERS OF EDINBURGH, AND A DIRECTOR OF THE SOCIETY.

To which are added

FACTS SERVING TO ILLUSTRATE

THE CHARACTER

OF

THE RIGHT HONOURABLE

THOMAS LATE EARL OF KINNOULL.

EDINBURGH:

AT THE Apollo Press, BY MARTIN AND M'DOWALL.

Anno 1788.

EDINBURGH, JUNE 5. 1788.

At a General Meeting of the Society in Scotland for propagating Christian Knowledge,

RESOLVED,

THAT the Thanks of the Society be given to the Reverend Mr John Kemp, for his excellent Sermon preached this day before them, and that he be requested to allow the same to be printed for the benefit of the Society.

JA. BONAR, *Clk.*

TO THE RIGHT HONOURABLE

ROBERT EARL OF KINNOULL.

MY LORD,

    AT the desire of your worthy and revered uncle, the following sermon was preached. I had repeatedly declined that office upon former occasions, but His commands to me were sacred, for they were ever reasonable and obliging.

    To him it was my original purpose to have asked permission to address it, not merely from the respect due to him as President of the Society, but from a more personal connexion, leading to warmer sentiments of gratitude. My obligations to that good man were great. He was my father's benefactor and friend. He distinguished me in early life by his kind notice,—to him I was indebted for my first preferment in the Church, and to him I was bound by his uninterrupted friendly regards, for near twenty years.

To him, for he seemed anxious to perpetuate to me the kindness of his family, I owe your Lordship's knowledge of me, and the polite attentions with which you have honoured me.—I am proud to embrace the opportunity which your permission has afforded me of publishing under the sanction of your name, my grateful sense of these singular favours.

It is the consolation of your country, my Lord, and it is mine, upon the loss of that venerable and good man whom you represent, that his successor has imbibed his spirit, and is ambitious of following his example.

And may you indeed, my Lord, walk in his steps.—May equal utility and equal honour mark the progress of your life, and in late old age, when it shall seem good to Divine Providence to call you hence, may your memory be

Opposition to the gospel, however, has not ceased: It has only assumed a different form, the more dangerous, perhaps, that it is disguised. Even among its professed advocates and defenders, there are not wanting some most unfriendly to those sublime and important truths, by which, as a system of religion, it is peculiarly distinguished.

These men, assuming it as a principle, that human reason is the sole judge of all objects of faith, make it their endeavour to bend Christianity into a compliance with the dictates of their own understanding. They fix the limits even of a divine revelation, and whatever exceeds the boundaries which they have marked out, they scruple not to reject as incredible, and impossible to have come from God.

Much learning and excellent criticism have been employed in defence of the ancient and generally received system of evangelical truth, and to prove that it is no less *really* than *apparently* contained in the word of God.

But, independent of the plain and direct testimony of scripture and just reasoning founded upon it, there is a test, by which doctrines claiming to be evangelical, may, and ought to be tried,—a criterion to which the advocates for human reason ought not to object, because at least to a certain extent, it accords with their own plan, and that is the standard of human nature; not, indeed, as it is exhibited in the fancied portraits of poets and philosophers, but as it is seen and felt in observation and experience.

Is the gospel, in the full extent and connexion of its doctrines, adapted to the state and circumstances of man? Is it fitted, with exquisite skill, to afford a supply to his wants, and a remedy to his intellectual disorders? Is its native tendency to elevate our species to a rank in the scale of moral excellence, far beyond what any other fyftem ever propofed or attempted? Then, from its own nature arifes an argument for its Divine Original, amounting almoft to demonftration; and every ferious candid enquirer will acknowledge with the apoftle, in the words of my text, that " *Chrift is the wifdom of God,*" or, in other words, that thefe doctrines, and that fyftem which have Chrift for their author and object, by their ftructure and tendency afford evidence of wifdom more than human, and could have proceeded only from God.

This is the fubject to which I wifh to direct the attention of my much refpected hearers, upon the prefent occafion. It is evidently an important theme. It places the fcheme of the gofpel, not perhaps in a new, yet certainly in a moft interefting point of light, and feems well adapted to the intention of our prefent affembly.

And if, upon a fair and candid examination, it fhall appear, that the gofpel is admirably adapted to the state and circumstances of man, to remove his disorders, to supply his defects, and to carry him forward to the highest improvement of which his faculties render him susceptible; then it follows, that, to convey the knowledge of that system to those of our fellow creatures, who either enjoy it not at all, or but in a very imperfect degree, is an undertaking benevolent and laudable; and that a society which have this for their object, are entitled to the approbation and countenance of their fellow citizens.

In the prosecution of this subject, I wish not to attempt a laboured argument addressed to the mere intellect: my appeal is to feeling and experience, as well as to reason. I wish my hearers to retire into their own bosoms, to attend to what passes there,—and there to suffer a plea in behalf of "Chrift, as *the wifdom of God*," to reach them.

Upon an attentive furvey of the natural ftate and circumftances of man, the following propofitions, it is imagined, will be found undeniably true.

Firſt, THAT man, altho' indued with the capacity of receiving information, yet, by his own unaffifted efforts, is totally unable to acquire the knowledge of thofe truths, with which it chiefly imports him to be acquainted.

Secondly, That, upon his being enlightened with the true knowledge of God, and of his duty, he muft neceffarily be impreffed with a deep fenfe of his own depravity and guilt.

Thirdly, That he has a confcioufnefs of moral obligation, and ideas of moral excellence, which from experience he finds he never can by his own efforts fulfil and attain.

Fourthly, That he is subjected to many afflictions, for which, upon the principles of reason, he cannot account, nor discover to what good purpose they tend.

Lastly, That, although he feels both presages of, and desires after a future state of being, yet, from the light of nature, he neither derives assurance of its existence, nor any certain information concerning it.

Let us consider these propositions, and enquire how far they are founded. If it shall appear that they are strictly true, then let us examine in what manner the gospel provides a remedy for the disorders, and a supply to the defects which they imply. The subject, I am sensible, is far too extensive for the limits of a single discourse; but it was the subject recommended for this occasion by a person to whom both the Society and the Preacher lie under many obligations,—a person whose extensive knowledge and deep sense of religion, vindicated by a corresponding practice, gave peculiar weight to his opinions, and recommendations in matters where religion was concerned; I mean our late noble and excellent President. Respect for the memory of this good man is my apology for entering upon so large a field. It is indeed but a small part of it over which I can hope to travel; but I may be able, perhaps, to point out to my hearers some paths by which, with much pleasure and advantage, it may be explored.

THE *first* proposition is, That man, though indued with a natural capacity of receiving information, yet, by his own unassisted efforts, is totally unable to acquire certain knowledge concerning those truths and objects, with which it is of chief importance for him to be acquainted.

The cause of human reason has been pleaded with ability and zeal; ingenuity and skill have been exhibited in the construction of beautiful systems of natural religion; the loveliness and obligation of virtue have been displayed in all the glowing colours of imagination and language. But these elaborate efforts in defence of the human understanding, it is to be observed, are, almost all of them, posterior, not only to the Christian æra, but to the period of the Reformation. What nature could, or could not have done, it is perhaps impossible for us, by an abstract investigation of the question to determine. But what she *has* done, and in the most favourable circumstances we certainly know, and the result affords no great room for boasting to her advocates.

Let us look into the state of religious knowledge among nations unacquainted with a divine revelation, not among the rude and barbarous, they might be deemed unfair examples; but in the philosophical and classical ages of Greece and Rome, when all the powers of the human mind were cultivated to a degree of perfection, which the efforts of modern times never can surpass. And yet in those refined ages, when science and art shone forth with a lustre which does honour to humanity, how gross and deplorable was the darkness of even the wisest of men with regard to the most important of all subjects, the nature and perfections of the Deity, the relations which man bears to God, and the duties which these relations infer? It were indeed highly unbecoming in us, who enjoy such superior advantages to affect to undervalue the ancients. In composition and reasoning, as well as in the fine arts, they will ever be regarded as models even to modern genius. And as to religion and morals, what labour and learning and ingenuity could do, they have done; yet how miserably they have failed is known to all who are converfant in their writings. Their ideas of God were vague, confufed, contradictory: To the rational homage, due to him as the Creator, Preferver, and Governor of the univerfe, they were ftrangers: Their fyftems of morals were confined and defective, being calculated rather for the forms of republican government, than for mankind at large; their profpects of futurity were dark and uncertain.

Thefe things, it were eafy to prove, by entering into a particular detail; they often have been proved to a demonftration; what then fhall we think of the modefty of modern advocates for reafon, who, while they pretend to reject the aid of divine revelation, lay claim to a knowledge in divine things, more accurate and profound than was ever poffeffed by a Socrates or a Plato, a Cicero or an Antoninus? This affumed fuperiority is an infult offered not to revelation only but to reafon itfelf.

But if men of profound intellectual abilities, whose whole time and attention were devoted to abstract speculations, were ignorant of the leading fundamental principles of religion, what must have been the situation of the great body of the people? *Them* the philosophers professed not to teach, *them* they regarded, and treated with the most sovereign contempt. The religion of the people was accordingly a motely composition of fable and superstitious absurdity. Their manners corresponded; and what hopes could be entertained of their reformation, while, in their most flagitious enormities, they were vindicated by the example of the gods, or rather the fictitious monsters of vice and impiety which they adored?

What then in respect of religious information constitutes the astonishing difference between them and us? Nothing it is obvious, but that written revelation with which God has blessed mankind in the scriptures: A system calculated for the instruction and moral improvement, not of the wise and learned only, but of the people at large, of mankind in all ages and nations; in every sphere and condition of life, and in every stage of intellectual improvement.

Our blessed Saviour and his apostles held no secret doctrines with mysterious caution imparted to their immediate disciples, and other doctrines, which they promulgated to the people. They addressed their whole system to the public, and in terms, which, while level to the meanest capacity, were calculated to enlighten the most profound. Hence we account for a fact the most extraordinary in the history of our species, that a Christian of the meanest station knows more of God and things divine, than all the wise and learned of Pagan antiquity. While they disputed concerning the being, perfections, and government of the Deity, and could agree upon nothing; the humble Christian mechanic knows and firmly believes in the one only living and true God, the Creator, Preserver, and moral Governor of the world.

While *they* doubted whether *any*, or what acts of devotion were proper, *he* approacheth with humble joy and confidence to the God and Father of the Lord Jesus in these exercises of his worship, which God himself hath prescribed.—While *they* removed God to an infinite distance from them, and resolved all events into an unintelligent blind fate, or into general undistinguishing laws of nature originally established; *he* believes and confides in the constant presence and influence of a kind over-ruling and particular providence.—While ancient philosophers debated concerning a state of future existence, leaning sometimes to the side of hope, but oftener far to that of doubt, and on the whole considered death rather as an eternal sleep, than an introduction to another mode of being; the Christian, learned in the scriptures alone, regards this life but as the commencement of his existence, and death as the gate through which he shall enter into mansions of immortal felicity and perfection.—While the disciples of nature could never conceive an idea so strange as that of the resurrection of the body, or so astonishingly grand as that of a general judgment; every real Christian's mind is established in the belief, that a day is approaching, when the whole human race in one vast assembly, and in both parts of their frame restored to union, shall stand before the tribunal of him who made them, shall each receive from his righteous sentence a portion suited to his real character, and be immediately sent into realms of eternal happiness, or regions of darkness and despair. What magnificent, what sublime ideas are these! How far beyond the reach of human discovery; and how powerful must be their influence upon every mind which sincerely believes them!

But it is not in these grand leading principles alone, that the naturally dark and benighted mind is illuminated by the gospel; no truth in religion or morals is left undiscovered which it is necessary or proper for man to know, and none, perhaps, which, in the present state of his faculties, it is possible for him to comprehend. Every thing is revealed which can serve to enlighten his understanding, with respect to the great principles of faith and duty, form his heart to the love of God and goodness, and train him up in a course of progressive moral improvement, into a fitness for being finally united with the Author of his existence.

These truths, permit me to observe, as a matter deserving particular attention, the Christian receives, not as probable conclusions from a train of reasoning, in which it is possible his own mind may have deceived him; he assents to them not with a faith, wavering at best, and always subject to the encroachments of doubt; he receives them upon the testimony and authority of God; he confides in them as truths, certain as his own existence, and which, even in his widest deviations from the plan of conduct they prescribe, it is impossible for him to reject. The *experienced* Christian, in giving credit to this divine system, rests upon evidence, which, though he cannot communicate it to other men, is to him demonstration; by its irresistible energy and happy influence upon his own heart and life, he knows and feels that it is *the power and the wisdom of God* for salvation.

Thus it appears evident, from the ignorance that prevailed in the most cultivated ages, that reason alone is a most insufficient guide to those truths which are of chief importance for man to know, that supernatural discoveries were absolutely necessary, and that in this respect the gospel revelation is admirably adapted to the circumstances and necessities of human nature.

This will appear no less evident from considering the

Second proposition, That the human mind, upon being enlightened with the true knowledge of God and of duty, must necessarily be impressed with a consciousness of guilt, and dread of punishment, for which reason and nature have provided no remedy.

That mankind in all ages, and under even the most imperfect notions and forms of religion, were affected with a sense of their own ill desert from a superior being or beings, appears evident from the whole train of their history. The great Author of nature never left himself without a witness in the human breast. The voice of conscience " *accusing or excusing*" too much accorded with the decisions of the understanding, to be wholly silenced by bad education, or corrupt systems of religion.

Yet it is certain that our ideas and our feelings of moral turpitude must always, in a great degree, depend upon the notions of duty which we have formed or received. It follows, therefore, that they whose minds, instead of being improved, were debased and corrupted by prevailing systems, must have felt comparatively but little uneasiness, in consequence of their deviations from the laws of genuine religion and of pure morality. Hence the idea of moral obligation, with the ancient Heathens, was the result of *feeling* rather than of reason; and their religious services the extorted drudgery of mercenary dread, rather than the voluntary tribute of reverence and love. It was chiefly their experience of *physical* evil which gave birth to their consciousness of *moral* guilt, it was when lightnings flashed and thunders rolled, when war and famine and pestilence spread devastation around, that they were terrified into the belief of having deviated from the will, and transgressed the laws of the God of nature. Hence their omens, their augurs and oracles, their priests and temples, and the whole costly train of their religious rites; hence in a a particular manner, their victims offered up in sacrifice to obtain the favour, or expiate the wrath of offended Deity.

Sacrifices, as has been often observed, afford the most unequivocal proof, not only that a sense of guilt and of deserved punishment, but also of the necessity of an atonement, were universal among mankind. At the same time, it must be admitted, that reason, in vain, seeks to find out a connexion between the shedding of the blood of an animal, and the remission of human transgression. With much probability, therefore, it has been concluded, that the idea of sacrifices originated, not from the natural deductions of reason, but from a divine revelation handed down by tradition. Yet still the universality of the practice, while other truths and ordinances of religion were totally obliterated and forgotten, amounts to a proof, that a sense both of guilt, and of the necessity of an atonement is congenial to the human mind.

If such was the general conviction of mankind, when guided by nature alone, and with such imperfect notions of God and duty as she afforded, what must be the ideas and feelings of men enlightened in the true knowledge of the Supreme Being, the extent and perfection of his laws, and the awful sanctions by which they are enforced? Many, it is admitted, acknowledge these truths, who are but little affected by their practical influence. When stimulated by the impulse of passion, reason, and argument, and even obvious interest plead with them in vain. It is not in the season of health and prosperity that we can expect, from a man of the world, serious attention to the representations of another, or even to the convictions of his own mind, concerning the depravity of his character. But visit him in the day of his calamity, when pain of body and anguish of spirit have taken hold of him. See him especially in the near views of death, roused to consideration of his spiritual and eternal state, forced to look back upon his past life, and forward to an awful futurity; ask him *then* how he is to appear before God, what account he can give of his life, and upon what grounds his hopes are founded? (No harm, but much good, may arise to each of us, from our sometimes, in imagination, placing ourselves in these circumstances, 'ere long they will be real to us all, and asking ourselves such interesting questions.)

The delusive hopes which ignorant superstition received from designing priestcraft, it is not necessary in this country and in the present age to expose. Excepting that of the gospel then, there are but two pleas, to which with any probability of success, man can have recourse; his own attainments in virtue; and the mercy of God. As to the first of these, the plea of merit; who, that is possessed of a sound mind, will, for a moment, rest upon it, as his title to eternal life? Examine the best of your actions, analyze the principles from which they proceeded, and on which they were conducted; bring them to the standard of conscience, compare them with the pure and spotless precepts of the gospel, you will find that they come far short, that they are full of imperfection.—But had the case been otherwise, and had a few actions of your life been perfectly pure and virtuous, still you are but *unprofitable* servants, and even in these have done no more than your duty. Surely, then, these can make no atonement for the innumerable transgressions which you must confess. The plea of merit, indeed, from a creature to his Creator, from a creature, especially, so guilty and depraved as man, is at once so arrogant and absurd, that stupidity and ignorance alone can urge it.

The other plea to which the sinner may have recourse,—*the mercy of God,*—is far more plausible; yet neither will this avail him, if raised on any foundation save that which God himself hath established in the gospel. In any other way it must be rejected as invalid both by reason and by conscience. For, the stern demand of reason is absolute, unlimited obedience; and the accusing voice of conscience fills the heart, not with the hopes of pardon and acceptance, but with the sad forebodings of impending judgment. What then is the ground upon which the light of nature can direct the sinner to build his hopes of the divine favour. It is, at least, but a faint probability, a presumptive hope, that in compassion to his weakness, God *may be* pleased to pardon his transgressions, and to accept of his services imperfect and unworthy as they have been. But this plea, it is evident, may be urged, and these hopes be assumed, by every offender, however enormous, against every law both human and divine, which is at once to annihilate all distinction between right and wrong, virtue and vice. If the extent of the divine favour is to be measured by the unbounded hopes of the sinner, then how are the perfections of Deity, and the equity of his moral government to be vindicated? How is a discrimination to be made between the righteous and the wicked, " between those who serve God and those who serve him not?"

Both reason and conscience concur in condemning the sinners' claim to the mercy of God: A claim suggested by audacious hope, and founded upon principles too fallible, to afford such security, as can bring peace to a mind anxious about futurity, and apprehensive of just retribution.

Now, if this sandy foundation be the only one upon which the religion of nature supports the hopes of her votaries, let us enquire, whether the wishes of the human heart be placed upon firmer ground, by the gospel itself, according to *a late fashionable system.* A system, of which the chief object is to exclude from revelation the atonement of Christ, that grand and capital doctrine, which hitherto, in the general sense of the church, was not only its characteristical distinction, but the great pillar on which all its other parts depend. To the abettors of this system, the doctrine of salvation by the cross, instead of the *wisdom of God*, appears, as much as ever it did to the ancient Jews

and Greeks, "*a stumbling block and foolish-*
"*ness.*"

To enter into the field of controversy upon this subject belongs not to my design: Nor is it necessary: Ability and learning and eloquence have been employed in its defence, at least in an equal measure to any which have been opposed to it, and with this singular advantage, that in the plain sense and common acceptation of words, the uniform language of scripture is decidedly in its favour. So much, indeed, is this the case, that great ingenuity and skill in criticism alone can torture them into a different meaning. " That Christ suffered and died as an a-
" tonement for the sins of mankind," says a late polite and ingenious lay-writer *,
" is a doctrine so strongly and so con-
" stantly enforced, through every part of
" the New Testament, that whoever will
" seriously peruse these writings, and de-

* Soame Jenyns.

" ny that it is there, may with as much
" reafon and truth, after reading the
" works of Thucydides and Livy affert,
" that in them no mention is made of
" any facts relative to the hiftories of
" Greece and Rome."

In behalf of this moft interefting doctrine, I would appeal, not merely to found criticifm and fair interpretation of fcripture; I wifh it to be tried not by the underftanding and the reafoning powers of the mind only, but alfo by the feelings of the heart, and particularly by the confcience of a finner awakened to a fenfe of guilt, and alarmed by the thoughts of a judgment to come.—Defcribe to a man of reflection, in that ftate of mind, the plan of the gofpel when ftripped of this doctrine; tell him of the fublimity of its doctrines, the purity and excellence of its precepts, and the awfulnefs of its fanctions; delineate to him the unexampled innocence and beneficence of the life of its blessed Author, the astonishing magnanimity and fortitude of his death, not as a *sacrifice for sin*, but as a *testimony to the truth of his doctrine and mission*: Explain to him, if he will listen to you, the laboured and ingenious criticisms by which you remove the common acceptation of words, and prove that the doctrine of the atonement has no place in the sacred page. But what, may not the alarmed sinner justly reply, does all this contribute to the ease and comfort of my troubled mind? The purity and extent of the system of duty enjoined by the gospel, its dreadful sanctions, and the sublime character of its Author as an example, only tend to exhibit in more glaring colours, the imperfection of my obedience, the greatness of my sins, my just desert of punishment, and my total incapacity of making any satisfaction to divine justice. *You* tell me, that even up-on *your* plan, the gospel contains the strongest assurances of mercy and pardon to the sincerely penitent. But does not the same gospel, in solemn terms, declare " That God is of purer eyes than to be- " hold iniquity, that he will not acquit " the guilty; that the unrighteous shall " not inherit the kingdom of God; that " he will render to every man according " to his deeds, indignation and wrath, " tribulation and anguish upon every " soul of man that doth evil." Some way there must be, if the gospel be indeed from God, of reconciling those contradictory assertions. Your hypothesis does it not. From it I derive no solid satisfaction to my mind. In it I perceive no foundation upon which I can build my hopes of pardon and acceptance with God in any consistency with his truth and justice, with the harmony of his perfections, and the equity of his government. On the contrary, by pointing out the purity and extent of the divine commandments, and the terrible punishments prepared for transgressors, it only serves to render my condition more hopeless and desperate.

To a person in this state of mind, what sounds can be so cheering, so full of consolation and peace, as those which convey the true and distinguishing doctrine of the gospel? " God so loved the world,
" that he gave his only begotten Son,
" that whosoever believeth on him should
" not perish, but have everlasting life.—
" Herein is love, not that we loved God,
" but that he loved us, and sent his Son
" to be the propitiation for our sins.
" There is now therefore no condem-
" nation to them that are in Christ Je-
" sus. It is God that justifieth, and who
" can condemn?"

Where was there ever a doctrine or an idea conceived or proposed, so wonderfully calculated to give ease to the soul trembling under a consciousness of guilt, as that which is contained in thefe, and a thoufand other paffages equally explicit? Are the difficulties, which the pride of human reafon fuggefts, unfurmountable obftacles to the reception of this doctrine? Shall we renounce, with difdain, that pardon of fin and that gift of eternal life, which nature moft vehemently folicits, becaufe offered not in the way which our fhallow underftandings propofe, but in that which infinite wifdom hath chofen, as the purchafe of the obedience and death of the Son of God?

In the page or field of controverfy, in the warmth of angry theological debate, and eager conteft for victory, objections may appear formidable. But what will be their afpect to the Chriftian, in his hours of retirement and ferious reflection, when meditating upon his own character and defert, and looking forward to his appearance in the prefence of his Maker? Then, be affured, thefe mountains created by pride and contention will dwindle away into nothing, and the mind will return to sentiments more becoming its condition. In these seasons, the questions which appear of chief importance are not, in what mysteries and difficulties is this doctrine involved, but, *are the scriptures the word of God?* and *is this doctrine of the atonement there plainly asserted and maintained?*

Mysteriousness undoubtedly attends it, but mysteries inexplicable occur in every fact which we observe in the natural world, and why should we presume to think that in a plan so grand and sublime as that of the recovery of a lost and perishing world, there should not be circumstances, which our very limited understandings cannot explain.

If satisfied that it is the doctrine of the word of God, the difficulties attending it, will be easily overcome; and with a grateful joy proportioned to its value, the humble Christian will accept of it " *as the unspeakable gift of God*" for salvation.

One remark, which the serious contemplation of this subject suggests, is of such importance as to deserve your particular attention; it is this: That the idea of God reconciling a lost and guilty world to himself through the medium of the obedience and death of his own Son, is in itself so sublime and so astonishing, so far removed from every thing which ever had, or could be supposed to have entered into the human mind, that this of itself affords a strong presumption, that from human invention it never originated. But now that it is revealed from God, what truth can bring along with it such peace and security to the heart? In the obedience and expiatory sacrifice of the Son of God, the true Christian sees not only all ground of fear removed, but the most sublime and satisfying prospects opened to his view, he beholds all the perfections of the divinity harmoniously engaged in his behalf, and the God of nature bearing to him the relation of a Father, in the most endearing sense of that expression. Full of this idea the Christian rises to an elevation of mind and character, of which otherwise human nature is incapable. Secured in the divine favour and protection, he feels himself excited to every thing great and noble in sentiment and action; and resting upon this foundation, he calmly but cheerfully looks forward to that solemn day which will dissolve his connexion with the world, and admit him into the immediate presence and enjoyment of his God.

If such are the happy effects of this doctrine, and such the consolation, which, in circumstances the most affecting, it brings to the human mind; if in passages, without number of the scriptures, it is most expressly asserted; nay, if it be indeed, what it appears to be, the cardinal point upon which the whole scheme of revelation turns; and, finally, if it not only gives no encouragement to relaxation of morals, but brings along with it, the strongest and most affecting motives to holiness and purity of heart and life; then, upon what principles can we account for that zeal, which, with indefatigable perseverance labours to banish it from the standards of our faith? Let it's enemies prove that it is productive of any mischievous consequences either to society or to the individual, and we will excuse their hostile attempts. On this point we appeal in its behalf to fact and experience. Look around you in life, my brethren, and say from your own observation, whether they who sincerely believe and confide in the merits of the Saviour for acceptance with God, are less peaceable, industrious, and useful than others, as members of civil society,—less faithful, laborious and respected as ministers of re-

ligion,—less conscientious and upright in business,—less attentive and affectionate in fulfilling the various duties of social and domestic life? You cannot say so; you know that the very reverse is the truth. It is impossible in the nature of things, but that it must be so, for the faith of this doctrine necessarily leads to the hatred of sin, the love and practice of holiness. " The grace of God, that bring-
" eth salvation, hath appeared to all men;
" teaching us, that denying ungodliness,
" and worldly lusts, we should live so-
" berly, righteously and godly in a pre-
" sent world *.

---

* Tit. ii. 11. 12. See also Rom. vi. 1. Ja. ii. 14, &c. A multitude of other passages to the same purpose occurs in the New Testament. Indeed, one great object of the apostle Paul, in all his epistles, is to shew the necessary and inseparable connexion between the sincere belief of this doctrine, and holiness of heart and life.

If this is the truth as seen in fact and observation, where is the benevolence or humanity of attempting to deftroy the peace and darken the profpects of thoufands of ferious and good minds, founded upon this doctrine? Could we fuppofe it even a dream, a mere phantom of the imagination, yet if it is not only harmlefs but beneficial, is there not cruelty in difturbing it, and in endeavouring to awaken the mind from its fancied fecurity, to fear and doubt and perplexity?— But let us not be too much alarmed; there is no room to apprehend that thefe efforts, however zealoufly conducted, fhall operate to any great extent, or that the now fafhionable hypothefis fhall be of long duration. Like many other opinions, which have had their fucceffive days of triumph in the Chriftian world, it will vanifh and be forgotten; other fyftems of error may follow, and for a time obtain, but truth is powerful and fhall at length prevail. When wearied with controversy and misrepresentation, men will have recourse to the scriptures in their plain and obvious meaning, as the only standard of faith, and as containing the only system of principles which is adapted to the state and circumstances of fallen and guilty man. Human pride will bend submissive before the oracles of divine wisdom, and the doctrine of salvation, by the cross of Christ, be received with joy as the *wisdom and the power of God.*

The *third* proposition mentioned in order to shew the peculiar aptitude of the gospel dispensation to the state and circumstances of man is, That he has a consciousness of moral obligation, and ideas of moral excellence, which experience tells him he never can by his own efforts fulfil and realize.

That man cannot attain to that excellence of character, of which his mind naturally forms the idea, is evident from fact and universal experience. The moral and religious systems of men, guided by the light of nature alone, we have already considered, and found them to be most defective and erroneous. The moral feelings of men, it is true, must correspond with their ideas of duty, and moral obligation. Yet limited and imperfect as were those of the ancients, we find many of the best and wisest among them, acknowledging the insufficiency of their own powers, and the absolute necessity of divine assistance, to carry them to the heights of even that virtue, of which they had formed the conception. Nay, it is well known to have been a maxim universally received even among the Heathens, that without the *afflatus*, or inspiration of the Divinity, nothing great in sentiment or action was ever attained by man *. Such is the natural inftinctive fenfe of the human mind, of its own weaknefs and conftant dependence upon God! But if fuch were the convictions of men whofe ideas of moral obligation were fo exceedingly imperfect, what muft be thofe, which the knowledge of the grand and perfect fyftem of duty enjoined by the gofpel cannot but excite? A fyftem which, taking its rife from God, includes every relation in which man is placed, and every duty which thefe relations infer, which extends even to the regulation of the fecret movements of the heart?

* *Hymn of Cleanthes, tranflated by Gilbert Weft, Efq.*
For nor in earth, nor earth-encircling floods,
Nor yon ethereal pole, the feat of gods,
Is ought perform'd without thy aid divine;
Strength, wifdom, virtue, mighty Jove, are thine.
     WEST's Works, Vol. II. p. 48.

The heroes of Homer and Virgil, it is well known, accomplifhed almoft nothing without the interpofition of fome deity.

Upon taking a serious view of this great plan of duty, and then comparing it with his own powers and capacities, who will presume to say that he is able to realize it in practice? Folly alone can give birth to so absurd and presumptuous an expectation. Every man of candour will feel and acknowledge the declaration of the apostle Paul, to be far more consonant to his own experience. *I see a law in my members, warring against the law of my mind, and bringing me into captivity to the law of sin; so that when I would do good evil is present with me**. " My reason sees and ap-
" proves that which is good, and which
" the gospel hath enjoined, but I feel its
" authority infinitely too weak to enforce
" its own decisions. Passion and tempta-
" tion lead me astray, and I yield obedi-
" ence to the law of sin, at the very time
" that my conscience dictates unlimited
" compliance with the law of God. In op-

* Rom. vii. 23.

" pofition to my better judgment I reject
" my lawful Sovereign, and obey a ty-
" rant and an ufurper. Though an ad-
" mirer of virtue, I am a pitiful flave to
" vice, and in every ftep of my conduct,
" my own mind witneffeth againft me.
" Wretched man that I am, who, or what
" can deliver me from fo deplorable a fi-
" tuation?" Nothing, fays the voice of his experience, nothing fay the convictions of his underftanding, but the power of that God, who originally gave him exiftence.

But however much the natural feelings of its neceffity may dictate a wifh for fuch aid, where, fave in the gofpel of Chrift, is there a fhadow of hope, far lefs fecurity, that it will be afforded? With what infinite fatisfaction then, will the ferious mind liften to the gracious declarations of the Son of God: " That he was mani-
" fefted not merely to expiate the *guilt* of
" fin, but to deftroy its dominion in the

"soul; not only to procure for man a title to the divine favour, but to qualify him for its enjoyment. He came to destroy the work of the devil"—to undo the unhappy effects of man's original apostacy; to remove that depravity of nature which it introduced; to restore to the soul those moral excellencies which constituted the image of its Maker; and to train up the man, in a progressive course of improving virtue, into a fitness for admission into a state of felicity congenial to his rational and moral capacities.

The immediate agent, by whom these grand and noble objects are accomplished, we are taught by the gospel, is the third of the sacred Three, who bear record in heaven; that blessed Spirit of grace, whom, under the character of the Comforter, Christ promised to supply the want of his personal presence, *to convince of sin, of righteousness and judgment,* and to lead men to the knowledge, love, and obedience of the truth. It is the general affertion of our Lord, that "except a man be born of the Spirit, he cannot enter into the kingdom of God *." It is by the fecret but effectual energy of this divine Agent, that an entire change is produced upon the natural difpofition, and a new character formed, of which the particular features are exhibited in the gofpel, and often defcribed by its minifters in the detail.

In general, the great work of the Spirit is, to enlighten the underftanding to difcern, and incline the will to confent to the pure and fpiritual fyftem of the gofpel: To give, to the decifions of the judgment, authority and force, and to fubject the affections and paffions to its controul: To preferve the powers of the mind in their due rank and fubordination, and direct them into the

* John iii. 5.

proper channel for promoting the great ends for which they were given,—the glory of God, and the eternal happiness of the soul. For this purpose we are taught, that when received into our hearts, he purifies them and renders them a fit habitation for himself; he assists our desires and endeavours after religious improvement, and renders effectual, for accomplishing the ends of their institution, all the ordinances of the gospel. He establishes our minds in the true knowledge and faith of divine truth; gives purity to our desires, spirituality to our affections, and fervour to our devotion. He affords direction in difficulties, comfort in affliction, defence against temptation: He gives to the conscience, that peace of God which passeth understanding; and which even the terrors of death cannot shake. His operations are silent and invisible, yet their effects upon the mind and character afford certain evidence of their existence;

and what thefe are the fcriptures have told us, "love, joy, peace, gentlenefs, mecknefs, goodnefs," and in a word, all the mild and amiable virtues which reftore in man the likenefs of his Maker, and form the Chriftian to the life of heaven even while on earth.

This doctrine has been objected to, on account of its myfterious and inexplicable nature. And in fo far as regards the *manner* of the Spirit's operations upon the human mind, it is admitted to be inexplicable. This is allowed by our Saviour himfelf in his converfation with Nicodemus[*]. But the difficulty of accounting for a fact, is no argument againft its actual exiftence; otherwife there is not one fact in the natural world which might not be difputed. We often know that there does exift a connexion between caufes and their effects, when the nature and manner of that connexion, and the reafon why the one fhould

[*] John iii. 8.

immediately follow the other we cannot explain. We know affuredly that in man, mind acts upon body, but how it does fo, reafon and philofophy will fcarcely pretend to tell us. If this fact then, however dark and inexplicable, muſt be admitted, why ſhould it be thought incredible, that mind ſhould act upon mind?—And prefumptuoufly to deny, that, that almighty Spirit who gave exiſtence to all other beings corporeal and incorporeal, who upholds and governs, who actuates and pervades the whole, cannot and does not act upon the human foul, is as little conformable to the expectations of nature and the dictates of found philofophy, as it is to the conſtant uniform language of fcripture.

It is farther objected, that this doctrine is inconfiſtent with the freedom of human agency: But, from confidering the nature and objects of the operations of the Spirit, the very reverfe appears to be the truth. He neither deprives the foul of any of its natural faculties, nor superfedes the use of them. He only preserves them in their just subordination, and gives to the understanding that authority and decision, which are necessary to its pursuing with freedom and effect, its proper objects. "If *he* worketh in us," it is only that "*we* may both will and "do that which is well-pleasing to God," and conducive to our own highest and best interest. And who is so free as he who feels himself emancipated from the shameful bondage of sin, and who has voluntarily engaged in the service of his Maker. "The man whom the Son of "God hath made free, must be free in- "deed."

Impious wits and libertines have presumed to exhibit this doctrine of the influences of the Spirit, in forms as ridiculous as they are profane. But by such attempts, they only expose the depravity of their own hearts, their ignorance of human nature, and their shocking ingratitude to God, for these much needed interpositions of his grace.

And now, let me ask, what there is, in the state and circumstances of man, which can vindicate the rejection of this most precious doctrine? Who can reflect upon the history of ages that are past, or look around him into real life at present, and observe the general prevalence of depravity and vice among mankind, together with the absolute inefficiency of ordinary teachers for their reformation, and not acknowledge the necessity of another and more powerful instructor? Or, who can attend to his own experience of the extreme imbecility of his nature, as well as the insensibility and averseness of his mind to spiritual and divine things, and not confess his entire dependence upon the grace of God, rejoice in the offers of it made in the gospel, and with earnestness, proportioned to the value of the gift, implore that it may be vouchsafed to him? As to the *real Christian*, he needs no other argument than his own experience. By the happy effects which he hath produced upon his heart and life, *the Spirit of God witnesseth to his spirit*, the certainty of his divine influences. They are the foundation of his confidence, the source of his comfort and hope. Conducted by this infallible guide, he trusts to be enabled to advance in those paths of pleasantness and peace, which lead to the mansions of eternal joy.

Thus, from the effectual aid which it affords, we discover, how admirably, in this respect also, the gospel is adapted to the circumstances and necessities of human nature.

The *fourth* proposition mentioned in order to shew the aptitude of the gospel to the state and circumstances of man is, That he is subjected to many unavoidable evils, for which, upon the principles of reason, he can neither account, nor discover any important good purpose to which they tend.

In no point of view, perhaps, does the gospel wear a more pleasing aspect, or appear more exquisitely suited to the necessities of our nature, and in none does it manifest a more glorious superiority over all the systems of reason and philosophy, than in the consolations which it affords to the afflicted mind. Comfort in affliction was one great object of ancient philosophy, to the attainment of which its most strenuous efforts were directed; but never did it more completely fail, or appear with a more mortifying inferiority. It was impossible that in this, attempt it could succeed. While ignorant of the true cause and origin of evil, while a stranger to the belief of a particular overruling Providence, but especially while destitute of all rational and well-founded hopes in the rewards of futurity, upon what bafis could philofophy rear a folid fabric of comfort? Its boafted confolations, accordingly, we find to be little better, than either unmeaning declamation, or the arrogant dictates of a pride that was never made for man. Bring them to the teft of real life and experience, and their emptinefs will immediately appear. Try the influence of any, or all of them united, to bring comfort to a man labouring under the complicated ills of pain, poverty, and grief; and judge by the effect. Tell him with one fect of philofophers, that thefe evils under which he groans, are in fact *no evils*, and are founded only in imagination; that in every fituation of human life, however wretched and miferable in appearance, and however deftitute of hope in a future ftate, ftill to the wife and good man, virtue is its own fufficient reward: Or, with another fect, tell him that the evils of life are merely *fortuitous*, the effect of blind chance, or of an undistinguishing irresistible fate, and that to repine is vain; can you think that assertions like these will soothe the anguish of an afflicted mind, will not every sufferer to whom they are addressed, regard them rather as insults added to his misery?

Compare, with these suggestions of philosophy, the clear and consistent, the grand and sublime consolations of the gospel; and upon the issue even of that comparison, I should willingly rest the argument for the truth and divine Original of our holy religion. In the discoveries of Christ and his apostles, what is there wanting, which the understanding requires, or the heart of man feels to be necessary for his comfort under affliction? In the gospel, we are taught to believe, that not by general laws originally established, but by a particular watchful administration, the Almighty presides over the universe;—that the care of this Providence extends not to great and important events alone, the interest of nations, or the rise and fall of states, but to every the minutest concern of the meanest individual,—that all being his creatures, are the objects of his care, and that the infinitude of their number produces no anxiety or confusion in the divine understanding. "Not a sparrow can fall to "the ground without his knowledge, and "even the hairs upon our head are all "numbered by him [*]."

In the direction of human affairs according to our Saviour's doctrine, nothing is fortuitous, or contingent, and nothing left to the uncontrouled operation of second causes. Means and their effects as well in the moral, as natural world are in the hands of the sovereign Ruler of the universe, and arranged by him, in that precise manner, which infinite Wisdom knows to be best calculated

[*] Matth. x. 29.

for promoting his own glory, and the general good of his intelligent offspring.

These are truths, as sublime as they are important, to which the understanding gives its willing assent, and on which it reposes with confidence and security. But our blessed Saviour hath given a still more pleasing view of divine Providence, and, a yet more comfortable direction to the faith of his disciples. He taught them to regard God as bearing to them the most amiable and most endearing character in which he was ever represented to man, even that of a Father tender and affectionate, taking a particular concern in all that regards them, ordering every circumstance in their lot, and causing even those dispensations of his Providence, which to them may appear most dark, or which they may feel most distressful, effectually to promote their highest moral improvement. " Let not your hearts be " troubled," said he to his immediate disciples in the hour of their sorrow, and the same exhortation he is to be considered as addressing to his faithful followers in all ages, " ye believe in God, believe also " in me." Read, my brethren, the consolatory discourse of which these words are the introduction, attend to the various sublime sources of comfort which are therein opened up, and by these specimens judge of the consolations which the gospel at large holds forth to the distressed. What simplicity, what majesty, what authority is conspicuous in every sentence of that admirable discourse! Who that is capable of relishing the beautiful and pathetic, or of admiring the grand and sublime can peruse it, in a serious and especially in an afflicted hour, without feeling the most lively emotions of hope and joy excited within him? Even taste and sensibility, abstracting from devotion, must lead to the acknowledgment, that this discourse could have proceeded from none other, than one who intimately knows the recesses of the human heart, and is able to afford a remedy to its heaviest woes?

To specify, in the detail, the various sources of consolation which the gospel exhibits to the Christian mourner, would require a separate discourse, or rather a series of discourses. The gospel indeed, to every one who seriously examines its nature and tendency, will appear to be what its name imports; *good news*, tidings of great joy to all people; but it is in an especial manner addressed to the poor, the persecuted, the afflicted; and to give them consolation and hope, is one of its primary objects. The office assigned to its divine Author in ancient prophetic description of his character, and which he both applied to himself, and literally fulfilled, was " to preach good tidings to the meek, " —to bind up the broken in heart,—to "comfort all that mourn*." "Come unto me all ye that labour and are heavy laden, and I will give you reft †," was his own kind and gracious invitation. And where can the toffed, perplexed, agitated foul find peace, but in the bleffed affylum which he hath opened in the gofpel.

For the greateft miferies to which human nature is fubjected,—*ignorance, confcious guilt, and moral imbecility*, we have already feen the noble and effectual remedies which it hath provided. And as to affliction arifing from other caufes, none can be fo fevere and oppreffive, as that a balance, and more than a balance to them is not afforded, by the doctrines, the promifes, and fublime profpects of the gofpel.

To go through the melancholy catalogue of human ills is needlefs; however varied and however aggravated, in the confolations of the gofpel a remedy is to

---

* If. lxi. 1. and Luke iv. 16. &c.   † Matth. xi. 28.

be found for them all. Of these consolations this is the sum.—Their father in heaven sends trials and afflictions to his people, because he loves them: He proportions the degree of their sufferings to what he knows to be necessary in order to carry forward their spiritual improvement: He encourages them to spread their wants before him, and enjoy the exquisite satisfaction of pouring out their complaints into his compassionate bosom: He affords the supporting aids of his grace, in a measure corresponding to the severity of their trials, and he gives them assurance, that, however afflictive and distressing, " they shall yet work out for " them a far more exceeding, even an e- " ternal weight of glory."

How cold and comfortless are the refined consolations of philosophy, in comparison of these noble and refreshing truths? It is impossible not to feel for those who had no better to produce.

When we see labour, ingenuity, and eloquence employed, by the great masters of reasoning in ancient times, upon this subject; when we behold them turning on every side for comfort, and laying hold of every circumstance which reason could suggest to reconcile them to the evils of life; and the result of their painful research to be only darkness, gloom, and uncertainty; we can scarcely help dropping a tear of pity over their unhappy situation. But, " Blessed are our eyes, for
" they see, and our ears, for they hear" what these great and wise men with transport would have seen and heard, but were not so highly favoured.

" Blessed art thou, O sincere believer
" in the gospel, for to thee, thy Saviour
" hath revealed all that is necessary to
" reconcile thee to thy lot, however pain-
" ful and distressing. Much thy heaven-
" ly father may call thee to suffer, in the
" course of his righteous administration;

" thy worldly poffeffions may take wings,
" and leave thee poor indeed; thy good
" name may be wrefted from thee by envy
" and mifreprefentation; thy friends may
" prove cold and treacherous, and death
" may tear from thee, thofe on whom
" thy heart leaned with fondeft affec-
" tion; but ftill if thou retaineft thy con-
" fidence in the doctrines and promifes
" of thy Lord, thou canft never be be-
" reaved of comfort." Thefe are confolations addreffed not to reafon and the
pure intellect alone, but to the ftrongeft
affections of the heart. Supported by
thefe, feelings may be oppofed to feelings;
fuch as are grateful and cheering, to
thofe that are difmal and fad.—The view
of futurity, in an efpecial manner, un-
folded by the gofpel, like the fun burft-
ing from behind a dark cloud, will dif-
fipate the gloom, and enliven the darkeft
fcenes of life. It will fmoothe the pillow
of a fick-bed, and reconcile the mind e-

ven to poverty and pain. It will bring compofure to the Chriftian when bidding a laft farewell to a dear departing friend; nay amidft the laft pangs of the diffolving frame, it will fuftain his fainting fpirit.

AND this naturally introduces the laft propofition ftated in order to prove the fitnefs of the gofpel to remedy the defects of nature, *viz.* That reafon unaided, affords no fixed principles upon which the belief of immortality can be eftablifhed. There is unqueftionably in the human mind, a capacity of extending its views beyond a prefent world, and the exercife of this faculty is ever accompanied with fecret prefages and hopes of future exiftence. Anxious wifhes and foreboding fears, it is true, do of themfelves afford no certain evidence of the prolongation of our being, yet it is an undoubted fact, that the belief of immortality in one form or other has prevailed among mankind in all ages and nations; among the ignorant and rude, as well as the informed and cultivated.

Whence hath it arisen? From the conclusions of reason and the deductions of argument? Such never was nor could be the source of any one *general* opinion or persuasion.——For *reasoning*, the great body of mankind have neither leisure nor capacity.——With abstract arguments they are totally unacquainted, and when proposed to them they have no force or effect upon their minds.——As to the immortality of the soul, it is certain, that so far was the belief of it from originating from learning and philosophy, that scepticism with respect to it never prevailed, till it became the subject of reasoning and argumentation.

We are forced, therefore, to seek for another and more probable source of this universal persuasion.——And no opinion, on this point, seems to be so well supported as that of those who maintain that the doctrine of immortality is co-eval with man himself, that it was conveyed to him at his creation, by the Author of his being, and handed down by tradition through successive generations.

Certain it is, that the farther we trace back the history of the human race, the deeper and firmer we find the belief to have been of this great principle of religion and morals.

But it is natural to suppose that all traditional knowledge, the farther it removes from its source, the more it will be corrupted in its purity, and impaired in its influence.

And such was the fate of the doctrine under consideration. It degenerated from age to age, till at length, about the time of our Saviour's appearance, it was clothed in such extravagant forms, and so disfigured by the absurdities of vulgar superstition or poetical fiction, that men of sense and reflection were ashamed to adopt it into their systems of belief. Unwilling, however, to renounce entirely the hopes of nature, philosophers enquired with unremitting study, what support and encouragement they could derive from reason itself, in behalf of an opinion so congenial to the noblest ambition of man.

To this most interesting subject, they appear to have given the whole force of their minds, and all their great powers of reasoning. Every argument which the nature and faculties of the human soul, and their ideas of Deity could suggest, were considered and weighed with all the attention and care which genius and unwearied application could inspire and bestow. And what was the result? Greater hesitation, doubtfulness, and perplexity, than existed before.

Nor would this appear in the least surprising, did the limits of this discourse admit of an investigation of the arguments, whether physical or moral, upon which they rested the proof of immortality.

Certain it is that they served not to bring conviction to the understanding, or to establish the minds of even those who employed them, in the belief of this great fundamental principle. This is admitted by an elegant modern historian, who will not be accused of prejudice against them. " The writings of Cicero," says he, " represent in most lively colours, " the ignorance, the errors, and the un- " certainty of the ancient philosophers, " with respect to the immortality of the " soul. When they are desirous of arm- " ing their disciples against the fears of " death, they inculcate as an obvious tho' " melancholy position, that the fatal stroke " of our dissolution releases us from the " calamities of life, and that they can no " longer suffer who no longer exist *."

* Gibbon's History of the Decline and Fall of the Roman Empire, Vol. I. p. 556. 4to. edit.

Compare this dark and difmal ftate of mind in the moft enlightened of men guided by reafon alone, with the clear views, undaunted fortitude, and affured hopes of the firft Chriftians in midft of the fufferings, dreadful to nature, to which they were expofed.

" We are troubled on every fide," fays the apoftle Paul of himfelf and his fellow difciples, " yet not diftreffed; we are
" perplexed, but not in defpair; perfecut-
" ed, but not forfaken; caft down, but not
" deftroyed ;——for we know, that if the
" earthly houfe of this tabernacle were
" diffolved, we have a building of God,
" an houfe not made with hands, eternal
" in the heavens †."

Contraft the fentiments of Socrates with thofe of that apoftle when placed in the fame circumftances, and mark the difference, " I am now ready to be offered up," fays St. Paul to Timothy, " and the time of

---

† 2 Cor. iv. 8, 9. and chap. v. 1.

"my departure is at hand. I have fought
"a good fight, I have finished my course,
"I have kept the faith. Henceforth there
"is laid up for me a crown of righteouf-
"nefs, which the Lord the righteous
"Judge will give me at that day*. For
"me to live is Chrift," faid he in another place, "and to die is gain †."

And fee in what fublime and animating ftrains he writes, not merely of the immortality of the foul, but of the refurrection of the body, and its exaltation to a pure and fpiritual mode of exiftence, exempt from fuffering and decay, and qualified for being the habitation of the foul perfected in holinefs and glory.—
"This corruption," fpeaking of the body, "muft put on incorruption, and this
"mortal fhall put on immortality,—then
"fhall be brought to pafs the faying that
"is written, Death is fwallowed up in
"victory.—O death, where is thy fting,

* 2 Tim. iv. 6. &c. † Phil. i. 21.

"O grave, where is thy victory!" But read the whole of the noble discourse upon this grand and interesting subject, contained in the fifteenth chapter of the First Epistle to the Corinthians, and then say whether such ideas concerning the invisible world, could ever have entered into the unassisted mind of man.

The contrast might be carried on to a great extent, but I shall solicit your attention to two other passages only, in which it is complete.

" I have great hopes," said Socrates to his judges, " that this sentence of con-
" demnation *may be* to my advantage.—
" For either in death all our sensations
" are extinguished, and then it is like
" the repose of a quiet sleep undisturbed
" by dreams; or else it is a departure in-
" to another state whether they who have
" left the world are already gone. *And*
" *if this be the case*, is it nothing, think
" you, to talk with Orpheus, and Mu-

"sacus, and Homer, and Hesiod? I
"could die many times to enjoy the
"pleasure of such conversations."

Who can read this passage and not feel for this wise and excellent Heathen, thus expressing the hopes of nature, and thus uncertain concerning their accomplishment.

But attend to the animated representations given by the apostle Paul of the sublime society, which heaven will afford to the Christian. He speaks of it with equal assurance, as if he and they to whom he addrest himself, had been already introduced into the bright assembly. "Ye
"are come unto Mount Zion, and unto
"the city of the living God, the heavenly
"Jerusalem, and to an innumerable com-
"pany of angels; to the general assem-
"bly and church of the first-born which
"are written in heaven, and to God the
"judge of all; and to the spirits of just

"men made perfect, and to Jesus the mediator of the new covenant *."

Such are the prospects which the gospel opens up, and such the hopes which it holds forth to animate the labours, to soothe the afflictions, and to support the patient perseverance in well-doing, of all who receive it as a rule of faith. Prospects these and hopes, derived not from the fallible conclusions of reason, not from the fond wishes of an aspiring mind, but founded on the testimony of the inspired oracles of God. Upon this immoveable basis rests the whole fabrick of our belief concerning the existence of the soul after death—the resurrection of the body—a day of general judgment—the future torments of the wicked, and the glorious immortal rewards of the righteous.

These grand and most affecting doctrines are revealed, not in the language of mere affirmation only, but in so great

* Heb. xii. 22. &c.

a variety of figurative animated reprefentations, as to convey to the imagination, as well as to the reafon and judgment the livelieft and deepeft impreffions of their truth and reality. They are confirmed by the moft folemn authority which heaven and earth could afford—by the declarations, by the death, and refurrection and afcenfion of God's eternal Son. And what can operate fo powerfully upon the human mind as thefe views of the moral government of God? What can ferve fo effectually to recal men from the grovelling purfuit of objects unworthy of their nature, and excite their moft vigorous endeavours for the attainment of thofe moral qualities which will furvive the ftroke of death, and conftitute the eternal felicity of intelligent beings?

Who can reflect in particular, upon that happy immortality which Chrift and his apoftles have defcribed as prepared for real Chriftians, and not conftantly difcern its wonderful aptitude to the desires and noblest ambition of our nature? In fine, who can seriously attend to that glorious system of which this is the grand object and final consummation, and not acknowledge from the warmest feelings of his heart, as well as the fullest conviction of his understanding, that it is the great truth of God for the improvement and comfort of man.

Having thus offered a very general illustration of the several propositions stated, permit me to give the sum of what has been said, in a very short abstract.

Is the mind of man, naturally ignorant, by its own unassisted powers totally incapable of discovering truths in themselves most important, and of most essential consequence for man to know? Behold the gospel, like the benign rays of the morning sun on the benighted world, illuminating his dark understanding, instructing him in every branch of knowledge necessary to inform his judgment, to improve his heart, and elevate his soul to that rank in the scale of moral existence for which it was originally designed.

Is man guilty and depraved, condemned by his own mind, and terrified with just apprehensions of future and deserved punishment? Hear the soul-reviving language in which the gospel addresses him. " Believe in the Lord Jesus Christ, and " thou shalt be saved *. There is no " condemnation to them who are in Christ " Jesus.—It is God that justifieth: who is " he that condemneth †?"

Is man not criminal only, and obnoxious to deserved punishment, but to every moral and good pursuit weak and impotent, incapable of loving and serving and enjoying God? See the gospel holding forth, to his acceptance, the secret but effectual energy of the divine Spirit, to

* Acts xvi. 31.   † Rom. viii. 1.—33, 34.

change his disposition, renew his nature, and by his blessing upon means adapted to the end, to train him up in a progressive course of moral improvement into a fitness for the eternal enjoyment of his Maker.

Is man by nature the child of suffering and the heir of sorrow, is he subjected to a constant succession of afflictions for which he cannot account, and under which he finds no effectual consolation? Listen to the gospel assuring and convincing him, that these trials are not only no *real* evils, but blessings in disguise, the medicine of the soul, and means in the hand of God, for purifying it from the dross of corruption, and preparing it for admission into the regions of eternal purity and peace.

In fine, are man's natural prospects beyond the grave covered with darkness which reason in vain attempts to penetrate, and is his mind, in consequence, filled with fear and perplexity? See life and immortality unveiled by the gospel, every thing discovered concerning a future and unseen world which it is necessary for man to know, or which it is probable he can comprehend: Every thing at least, which can serve to allay his fears, confirm his hopes, and establish his mind in security and peace.

Consider then, this grand and wonderful system of divine wisdom and grace. Think of it with the seriousness which is due to the importance of the subject; view it in its full extent and beautiful connexion of parts;—then turn your attention upon your own situation and character, lay your hands upon your hearts and say if you can, that this is *not* the system which your nature required: Or rather say, whether it is possible for the human mind to form the conception of a scheme of religion, so admirably calculated to supply its defects, to heal its dis-cases, to restore it to its primitive dignity and excellence. Indeed, my friends, to the state and circumstances of man it is adapted with such perfect and peculiar skill, that to the mind which seriously attends to both, and compares them together, this conclusion is irresistible, " the " author of our nature, and the author " of our religion is one."

Let us now attend for a little to the improvement to be made of this discourse.

And, in the *first* place, let me ask whether this œconomy of religion is not worthy of all acceptation, as the noblest and best gift which heaven in mercy could bestow upon man? If so, how enormous is the guilt of these men, who, in spite of evidence the most satisfying, and too often, it is to be feared, in opposition to the convictions of their understandings, and the feelings of their hearts, not only reject this divine system, but traduce its excellence, hinder its progress, and strive to destroy its influence? Let them beware: Their guilt is great, their danger is extreme. "There is a sin which is unto death*; a sin which shall not be forgiven either in this world, or in that which is to come †."

In the *second* place, from the sketch that has been given of a few of its leading features, it appears, that the gospel contains an uniform, regular, and harmonious plan, so intimately and essentially connected in all its parts, that not one can be taken away, without a material injury to the whole. The grand object of the gospel, as we have seen, is to raise man fallen and apostate, from ignorance, guilt, and misery, to glory and immortality. The means employed are worthy of the end, they are alike from God, and their success is infallibly certain: for what infinite wisdom hath devised,

---

* 1 John v. 16. † Matth. xii. 32.

omnipotent power is able to accomplish. To alter, or innovate upon this plan, and especially to remove any one link of this great chain is dangerous in the extreme. Strip the gospel, for example, of the doctrine of the atonement, and what foundation remains to the sinner, on which to build his hopes of pardon and eternal life? Remove the influences of the Spirit, and how is it possible, that a being so depraved, so unlike to God, and so feeble in his moral and religious faculties can become qualified for the presence and enjoyment of his Maker? Take away any one doctrine peculiar to the gospel, and you destroy the unity and harmony of the whole system. It becomes broken and disjointed in its members, the means cease to be equal to the end, the soul is deprived of the great sources of its security, and relapses into fearfulness and doubt. In a word, it is no longer the plan of divine wisdom, but of human invention, nor is the honour of the divine perfections concerned to crown it with fuccefs.

Do you wifh then, my friends, to have your minds eftablifhed in the true knowledge and faith of the gofpel-fyftem? Seek it not, I befeech you, in the partial, infidious reprefentations of defigning men, but in the fcriptures themfelves. There you will fee it in all its excellence, you will admire its apitude to your condition, you will feel its vaft importance and value; and with joy you will acquiefce in it as the *wifdom and the power of God* for falvation.

Laftly, If the plan of the gofpel, in its true extent, be indeed fo admirably adapted to the ftate and circumftances of man; if it provides a remedy for his ignorance, guilt and imbecility; if it affords to him, the only effectual confolation under the various troubles and forrows of a prefent life, and the only fure foundation upon which his hopes of another and better can rest; then it follows, that to extend the knowledge, and to promote the influence of this divine system, are the noblest objects of human benevolence.

To a dark and benighted world at large, our efforts cannot extend. New arrangements of Providence alone, can pave the way for its conversion. But while we feel for the unhappy situation of the vast multitudes of our fellow creatures remaining in ignorance and idolatry, and lament our incapacity to bring them relief, let us humbly and earnestly recommend them, to the compassionate regards of the great universal Parent; let us plead with him as arguments, his respect to his own glory, and to the best interests of his rational offspring: Let us plead with him his own truth and faithfulness in fulfilling his promises, that by methods known to his infinite wisdom, he would enlighten the dark places of the earth, with the pure light of evangelical truth, and hasten the happy time foretold, " *when the dominion of Christ shall extend from sea to sea, and from the river even unto the ends of the earth *.*"

But although, by good wishes and prayers alone, we can express our Christian benevolence to the Infidel world at large, yet in behalf of certain corners of it, we may certainly employ more active and immediate exertions. To the remote, uncultivated, untutored districts of our own country in particular, we may, and every principle of religion, and every feeling of humanity call upon us, to send relief by such means as are within our power. *This is the well known object of that Society on whose account we have met together, and at whose desire I have addressed you.* Their panegyric would come with an ill grace from one of their own body, and who for

* Zech. ix. 10.

some years has had a share in the direction of their business.

A more particular account, than would become this place, of our procedure, of the special objects of our attention, and of the success which has attended our labours, will soon, according to usual practice, be submitted to the inspection of the public.—In general, I have the satisfaction to inform you, that, at no period, were the affairs of the Society in a more flourishing situation than at present,— at no period did they exhibit a fairer prospect of increasing benefit to our country. With the most lively gratitude, we acknowledge the continuing generosity of the public, and the munificence of individual benefactors, in consequence of which, from small beginnings, our funds have arisen to their present magnitude. Of the confidence of the public in the integrity with which this sacred and important trust has been conducted, we have received, and particularly of late, the most flattering and substantial proofs. Men of the first rank in the kingdom, whose names are an ornament to their high station, and others both of this and the neighbouring country, distinguished by the eminence of their talents, and their influence in public affairs, have not disdained to enrol their names with ours, as members of an association for promoting religious knowledge, and useful industry. They have not been ashamed to appear, in an open, avowed manner, as its patrons and benefactors, and with an active and liberal spirit, to labour for promoting its great and beneficent purposes. In the consciousness of their own benevolence, in the blessings of them who were ready to perish for lack of knowledge, and above all, in the approbation of the great universal Parent of mankind, may they find their noble reward!

To a variety of persons, whom their situation in life precluded from personal services, we have lately been indebted for generous donations, to assist in carrying on the good cause in which we are engaged. With gratitude they have been received, and with fidelity, they shall be employed.

But one donation received since we had last an opportunity of meeting together upon this occasion, is of too great magnitude to be past over, with this general acknowledgment. I mean the princely benefaction of a Lady*, whose name will long be precious to the real friends of religion and their country—a Lady whose rank and high connections, whose uncommon natural abilities, and acquired accomplishments, would have attracted the notice and commanded the respect of the politest circles, but whose chief distinction arose from a warm and uniform sense of piety, a heart-felt zeal for the best interests of

---

* Lady Viscountess Glenorchy.

religion and her fellow creatures, and unwearied, uninterrupted exertions in promoting them. To these important purposes she devoted her eminent talents and her beneficent life. To these objects, at her death, she confecrated her ample fortune: To promote the ends of this Society in particular, she bequeathed a sum* so confiderable, as greatly to enlarge our sphere of usefulness.

While we gratefully acknowledge this and other benefactions, while we give thanks to God, for putting it into the hearts of those to whom he had given the power, to bestow them; we at the same time profefs ourselves to be only stewards for the public, in employing them. For public purposes they were given, and to the public, we pledge ourselves, they shall faithfully be devoted. Be ours the pains and the labour, be theirs the advantage. We solicit the countenance and aid of our

* L. 5,000 Sterling.

fellow citizens, only in so far, as our fidelity to our trust shall appear to deserve them. The real friends of religion and their country must be friends to our cause. They who have seen the excellence and felt the power of the gospel of Christ, must be anxious for its extension; their hearts will dictate a benevolent, fervent prayer to the Father of Lights, that the glorious Sun of Righteousness may speedily arise upon the dark places of the earth; that upon the remote corners of our own country in particular, where as yet he is seen but obscurely, his light may break forth in all its lustre, to dispel the gloom of spiritual darkness, and to alleviate the wretchedness of penury and toil.

Real Christians cannot fail to regard with approbation attempts to open up prospects of present comfort, and of future joy to our unhappy fellow subjects, hitherto left in ignorance and poverty, to convey to them that peace and animating hope, which the benign influence of the gospel never fails to inspire. To such benevolent efforts, in their several stations, and according to their respective abilities, they will lend their countenance and aid, and to all they will join their earnest prayers for that blessing which alone can give success.

PRAY brethren for us, and for all who are immediately engaged in promoting the great objects of this institution, that our zeal and abilities may correspond to the importance of our work, that the effectual energy of the Spirit of God may accompany our endeavours, and that *we*, however mean and unworthy, may be honoured *as fellow labourers together with God*, to bring many souls from darkness and ignorance, to knowledge and light and life in the Lord. AMEN.

FACTS SERVING TO ILLUSTRATE

THE

CHARACTER

OF

THE RIGHT HONOURABLE

THOMAS EARL OF KINNOULL,

LATE PRESIDENT OF THE SOCIETY IN SCOTLAND

FOR

PROPAGATING CHRISTIAN KNOWLEDGE.

PUBLISHED BY ORDER OF THE SOCIETY.

EDINBURGH:
AT THE Apollo Press, BY MARTIN AND M'DOWALL.
Anno 1788.

THE CHARACTER

of

THE RIGHT HONOURABLE

THOMAS LATE EARL OF KINNOULL.

The Society in Scotland for propagating Chriſtian Knowledge, deeply ſenſible of the loſs which they have ſuſtained by the death of the Right Hon. Thomas Earl of Kinnoull, their late worthy Preſident, conſider it as a duty incumbent upon them to teſtify to the world their reſpect for his memory, and their gratitude for his beneficent attention to the objects of their inſtitution. As a Society, founded for the purpoſe of promoting the cauſe of religion, they think themſelves called upon, to exhibit to public view a character formed upon religious principles, and affording a bright example of their influence.

General panegyric is often the creation of fancy.—The object which they have in view, they imagine will be best attained, by a plain unornamented detail of a few facts in the conduct of this singularly good man—from these his real character will best appear.

The late Earl of Kinnoull was born in 1710, married 1741 to Constantia, daughter of John Kirle-Earnley, Esq;* by whom he had issue one son who died an infant. He was chosen Member of Parliament for Cambridge in 1741, and represented that Corporation till he succeeded his father in the Peerage in 1758. He was also chosen Recorder of Cambridge and held that office till his death. He was for many years Chairman of the Committee of Privileges. In 1741 he was appointed one of the Commissioners of the Revenue in Ireland,—in 1746, a Lord of Trade and Plantations,—in 1754, a Lord of the Treasury,—in 1755,

* She died in 1753.

Paymaster General of his Majesty's Forces, —in 1758, Chancellor of the Dutchy of Lancaster, and Member of the Privy Council,—and, in 1759, Ambassador Extraordinary to the Court of Portugal.

A representation of his conduct in public life is not intended by the Society, this they leave to be sought for in the annals of his country. Suffice it in general to say, that, guided by the purest principles of the constitution, he uniformly exerted himself to preserve inviolate the just rights and privileges of each part of the British legislature, to maintain the laws and liberties of his country, and to promote, as far as lay in his power, the safety, the honour, and the welfare of the state.

His unremitting attention to public business for so long a period, and in so many different offices, having greatly impaired his health, in 1762 he resigned all his employments under the crown, and resolved to dedicate the remainder of his life to retirement, at the seat of his ancestors.—A resolution, from which the most urgent solicitations and splendid offers were never able to divert him.

In January 1768, this Society, with one voice, invited him to be their President. An office for which he was eminently qualified, and which, with much credit to himself and benefit to the institution, he sustained till his death.

A liberal annual donation was but one of many favours which he conferred upon the Society. From the time of his election he entered with spirit and zeal into their objects, and uniformly exerted himself to promote them. When present, he presided with ability and moderation in their councils; and when absent, replied with scrupulous punctuality to their letters, and favoured them with his advice and assistance whenever they were requisite.—To his talents and influence, as well as to his extensive knowledge and long practice in business, the Society were often singularly indebted.

But his conduct, as president of this Society, exhibits only a partial and very limited view of this worthy nobleman.

His character was uniform and consistent in all its features, for it was formed by principles which admit of no variation. The Society can trace it only in a few of its outlines; but what they advance rests either upon facts of public notoriety, or the personal knowledge of some of their own members whose testimony is beyond suspicion.

A *warm but rational piety* was the great leading principle of his character, it directed and pervaded every part of his conduct in public and private life.

He made no ostentatious display of religion, but he was not ashamed to practise the duties, and avow the feelings which belong to a Christian. The apprehension of censure or of ridicule from the fashionable world, deterred him not from giving regular attendance upon the public ordinances of divine worship. This part of his conduct flowed from noble and just principles.

Public homage, he considered to be indispensably due from every member of society, to the great Author of all *public* as well as private good. He firmly believed in the established religion of his country. He felt the reverence which a good citizen owes to its institutions. He knew the influence of the example of men of his rank, upon the manners of the inferiour, and great body of the community. His attendance, therefore, upon public worship, was not occasional but regular, and extended to the whole of its usual and stated services.

Although, while resident in England, and in a public station abroad, he was of the communion of the Church of England, (naturally led to this, by his education and the practice of his family) yet when he came to live in this country, he conformed to the usages of the Church of Scotland. He well knew, that in articles of faith and doctrine, the two sister churches are united, and that matters of form constitute the chief, if not the only difference between them.

This good man's deep-felt sense of religion was expressed in a manner still more singular, and worthy of admiration.

When, from the absence or sickness of the minister, or any other cause, there was no public worship in his parish-church, it was his regular practice on the Lord's days to call together his family and domestics, to read to them a portion of the scriptures, and such books of religion as he judged best adapted to their improvement, and to preside among them in immediate acts of devotion.—And this last he uniformly did every Sunday evening through the year.

It was his opinion, that no elevation of rank can be an apology for the neglect of the duties which man owes to his Maker; and besides, that no man can ever appear in a more dignified or graceful attitude, than when at the head of his family, acknowledging the bounties, and soliciting the continuing protection of their great common Parent. The compositions which he used in these acts of family-devotion were his own, and singularly excellent,—in reciting them, which he did from memory, the animation and fervour of his manner at once demonstrated the warmth of his own devotional feelings, and excited a congenial spirit in the breasts of all who heard him.

When no clergyman was present, he always officiated as chaplain at his own table, both before and after meals,—not by the short form commonly, and too often irreverently repeated, but by a few suitable expressions pronounced with the decent solemnity which becomes an immediate address to the Deity.

He regularly joined in the celebration of the Lord's supper, in his parish-church, and attended upon all the religious services preparatory to, and consequent upon that ordinance, as usually observed in the Church of Scotland. The closeness of his attention, and the seriousness of his mind upon these occasions, visibly appeared in his countenance and manner. He had a singular delight in that ordinance, and it always seemed to produce the happiest effect upon his mind,—to give a brisker flow to his spirits, and a new degree of vivacity to his conversation.

The duties of the closet he observed with no less care than those of the family and church. To secret devotion a considerable part of his time was daily allotted; during the time consecrated to this purpose, no engagements in business, nor hurry of company were suffered to intrude. The scriptures were the guide and constant companion of his devotions. Few had studied them with closer attention, and few had more thoroughly imbibed their spirit.

His belief of Christianity was sincere, the result of serious and careful investigation. Almost every book of character, upon the nature and evidences of the gospel he had read with care, and as his memory was retentive to an uncommon degree, he was never observed to be at a loss when any branch of that subject was introduced into conversation.

Sincere in his profession of religion, every thing immediately connected with its interest engaged his attention. He was, of consequence, a friend to its ministers. They were acceptable guests at his very hospitable table, and with the worthy and learned among them he cultivated habits of familiar intercourse.

Some of the brightest ornaments of the Church of England he numbered among his particular friends; and of the Scottish clergy there were not a few whom he honoured with distinguishing marks of his confidence and esteem. To the ministers in his immediate neighbourhood, he gave a general invitation to his house, and to the use of his library; and encouraged them upon every occasion of moment, to solicit, and repose upon his advice and assistance.

In all those parishes where he was an heritor, he promoted the augmentation of the livings, and gave liberal assistance to every plan proposed for the accommodation of the ministers.

As he invited the clergy to his society and table, so there was not only nothing to deter, but every thing to induce them to comply. In his presence nothing was ever permitted which had the remotest aspect of indecorum, and such was the reverence which his well known character inspired, that even men of rank, tho' free in their principles, and in other companies licentious in their converfation, yet before him were moſt guarded and attentive to propriety.

But the Earl of Kinnoull's converſation was not innocent only, it was inſtructive in no common degree. Few men had treaſured up ſo great a ſtore of various and important knowledge. He was an excellent claſſical ſcholar, and while among literary men, his frequent and apt quotations, ſhewed his familiarity with the beſt writers of antiquity, particularly the Roman poets.

With the hiſtory and ſtate of modern literature alſo, his acquaintance was extenſive and accurate. The beſt new publications were regularly ſent to him, and added to his ample collection; they were frequently the ſubjects of his converſation, and upon none did his memory, taſte, and judgment, appear to greater advantage.

Another line of converſation in which he excelled, and for which he had an inexhauſtible fund of materials, was in giving curious and intereſting anecdotes concerning the diſtinguiſhed perſonages of his time, the political tranſactions of that period, and the ſecret ſprings which produced them.

The high offices of ſtate which he had long filled, and the habits of intimacy in which he had lived with people of high rank and conſequence, gave him opportunities of knowing, and entertaining his friends with many facts and circumſtances which they could derive from no other ſource of information.

His near relation to Robert the great Earl of Oxford, ſufficiently accounts for his early introduction into the political world; his own ability, integrity, and unremitting attention to buſineſs ſecured and increaſed that influence which naturally aroſe to him from his high connexions. With the first men of his time, both in the political and literary world, he lived in habits of familiar intercourse. Lord Hardwicke, Mr Pelham, the Earl of Mansfield, Archbishop Secker, and Mr Pope, were of the number, and may serve as a specimen of those with whom he chiefly associated.

A considerable part of a lifetime spent in such society, in scenes of national business, and in literary pursuits, could not but afford ample store of valuable information, nor, with his frankness of communication, fail to render his conversation as entertaining as it was instructive.

But the Earl of Kinnoull was not fitted only to shine in conversation,—he was still more distinguished by his active, diffusive benevolence. His retirement from public business was not devoted to indolence and inaction. The remainder of his life, though in a more contracted sphere, was affiduoufly employed in the fervice of his fellow creatures.

Many evidences of his public fpirit and beneficence he has left behind him. That noble and ufeful work the bridge over the Tay at Perth, it is well known, owes to him its exiftence,—under his aufpices, and at the rifk of his private fortune, it was reared, and will, it is to be hoped, remain to fucceeding ages a monument to his honour.

At the meetings of the noblemen and gentlemen of that part of the country where he refided, he gave conftant attendance, when his health permitted, and the importance of the object required his prefence. In their deliberations, the generofity and difintereftednefs of his views, united to his great talents and experience in bufinefs, never failed to command univerfal refpect.

The benevolent and worthy part which he acted towards the Society in Scotland for propagating Chriſtian knowledge, has been already mentioned. To various charitable inſtitutions in England, he was a a regular and liberal contributor.

But, in no part of his conduct did the excellence of this good man's heart more amiably diſcover itſelf, than in his behaviour to young people. An old man ſurrounded by young men ſtrongly attached to him, affords a pleaſing ſpectacle. It was the picture frequently exhibited by the Earl of Kinnoull. He delighted in their ſociety. He encouraged them to come to his houſe—ſuperintended their education—examined into their progreſs, and gave them inſtruction. He ſtrove, by every winning art and proper indulgence to make himſelf agreeable to them, and to gain their confidence, that he might improve their minds by uſeful knowledge, and form them to the love of religion and virtue.

With thefe difpofitions it is not to be wondered, that he accepted with pleafure of the office of *Chancellor of the Univerfity of St. Andrews*, to which, upon the death of the late Duke of Cumberland, the former Chancellor, he was unanimoufly elected in the year 1765.

Having made himfelf mafter of the hiftory and conftitution of that ancient feminary, he was enabled with knowledge and effect to interpofe in its affairs; and to every reafonable propofition for its advancement, he always gave the moft decided fupport.

The profeffors, encouraged by his engaging manners, regarded him as their friend, as well as patron, and were accuftomed in all their affairs of confequence to repofe upon his advice.

For the encouragement of genius and literature among the ftudents, he inftituted, at his own expence, annual premiums for thofe who fhould excel in the different claffes, and various branches of fcience. At the diftribution of the prizes he attended in perfon.

Upon a particular and ftated day, he went annually to St. Andrews, in his public character as Chancellor, and was received by the whole members of the univerfity, as well as many of the neighbouring gentry and clergy. In a full affembly, the young men, to whom the fuffrages of the profeffors had adjudged the preference, recited their feveral exercifes, and received from the noble Chancellor, the applaufe, together with the premium to which merit had entitled them. To this employment, as grateful to his own feelings, as well intended for the benefit of the public, he commonly devoted a week at a time.

During this annual vifit to St. Andrews, he never failed to witnefs, and to prefide in a public examination of the grammar-fchool. The warm applaufe which he bestowed upon the ability and success of the rector*, the animating encouragements which he held forth to the boys, and the satisfaction which glowed in his countenance on discovering, from year to year, their rapid improvement, marked the sincerity and ardour of his zeal for the good education of youth, and their progress in useful and polite literature.

But his attention to literary merit was not confined to honorary marks of his approbation. To genius and desert he always gave encouragement suited to the situation in which he found them; to young men of fortune his countenance and praise;—to those blessed with talents, but struggling with poverty, the means of carrying forward their education. And this he did, sometimes by procuring for them *Bursaries*, (corresponding to what in the English universities are called *Exhibitions*)—sometimes by occasional pre-

* Mr Halket.

fents of money and books, and fometimes by annual penfions. Even when their education was completed, he deferted not thofe whom he had affifted, or of whom he had conceived a favourable opinion— he exerted himfelf to obtain for them a comfortable fettlement for life. For fuch of them as had turned their views towards the church, he had opportunities of providing, by the number of ecclefiaftical benefices in his gift. And in this *capacity of patron of church preferments*, the piety and benevolence of his character receive a new and ftriking illuftration.

The Earl of Kinnoull was too well acquainted with human nature, not to be convinced that a favourable opinion of the teacher, upon the part of thofe whom he is appointed to teach, is as effential to his ufefulnefs among them, as it is to his own perfonal comfort. He had ftudied the genius of the people of Scotland, of that part of it in particular, where his intereft lay, and he knew how much of their happiness depends upon their having ministers possessing their confidence and respect established among them. He considered, moreover, the power of appointing the public teachers of religion as a sacred trust, which with conscientious fidelity it behoved him to fulfil.—To conduct himself upon these principles, was his uniform endeavour, and his success corresponded to the purity of his intentions.

Peace to the parish, and usefulness to the minister, were his great objects; yet he never suffered himself to become the dupe of either unmerited popular favour, or causeless popular resentment.

The maxim by which he conducted himself, in this part of his duty, will best appear in his own words, which he often repeated to his friends. "I will never," said he, " promote a clergyman of whom " I have not a good opinion, however

" earneftly the people may defire it, nor
" will I force even a good man into a pa-
" rifh, againft whom the parifhioners
" feem to have conceived invincible pre-
" judices."

In compliance with this principle, he fometimes found it neceffary to give way to a general oppofition from a parifh, to the man of his choice; but this was an exercife of moderation and prudence which he had feldom occafion to employ. Temporary difgufts againft deferving candidates, and the factious oppofition of popular demagogues, he knew how to overlook, or, by the weight of his authority and influence, to crufh. And fo fuccefsful was this plan of procedure, that during the whole courfe of his refidence in this country; and among many vacant parifhes fupplied either by his immediate patronage, or influence, there was not one which did not eventually prove comfortable, moft of them from the beginning were acceptable and harmonious.

As the Earl of Kinnoull was a friend to the clergy, and to the religious interests of the community, *so he was a liberal benefactor to the poor.* His private charities were many, some of them splendid; but over this part of his conduct he was careful to spread a veil; and as few of these good deeds as possible he suffered to be known, even by his friends.

With respect to the supply of the poor in general, he proceeded upon fixed and excellent principles. He judged it a better species of charity, to *prevent*, as far as it could be done, than to *relieve* necessities; he gave encouragement, therefore, to every species of useful industry among the poor, and to numbers of them, employment and bread.

To common begging he was a decided enemy; and to prevent the necessity of it, always declared that every parish ought to maintain its poor in their own houses. To assist the several parishes in which his estates lay, in accomplishing this object, he sent to each of them annually a stated sum, corresponding to the number of its poor, and the extent of his property. He thought it unreasonable and unjust, to carry his rents out of a parish, and leave the whole burden of supporting the poor upon the tenants; a practice too common in Scotland, where the poor, are in many parishes, left to be maintained by the contributions of their neighbours, sometimes only less poor than themselves. Were Lord Kinnoull's principles to be adopted, and his example to be followed, begging would be unknown, poors rates unnecessary, and the poor equitably and sufficiently provided for.

If we view this good man in the capacity of a *Landholder*, connected with a numerous body of tenants, his judgment and prudence will appear no less conspicuous, than his benevolence and humanity. He proceeded upon the maxim, that to confult the comfort and profperity of his tenants, was the fureft means of promoting his own intereft. He caufed proper plans of agriculture to be fuggefted to them, by perfons in whofe fkill he had confidence;—gave them leafes of a proper length and at moderate rents, and built houfes for them in a ftile far fuperiour to any that had been ufually given to farmers in that part of the country. He taught them to refpect themfelves as free-born Britons, and to repofe with unlimited confidence upon their mafter's honour and regard to their intereft.

Under his judicious management, his eftate fpeedily affumed a new face; improvements rapidly advanced, and his tenants profpered. Inftead of concealing, they were happy to avow to their kind mafter, their improving circumftances, for they knew that no undue advantage would be taken of the knowledge of them. They regarded him as their common father, ever attentive to their situation, anxious to redress their grievances, and to promote their prosperity.

A more particular account of his conduct as a landholder, might afford much pleasing, as well as useful information, but besides that this is less immediately the object of the Society, it would lead to too great prolixity. Suffice it therefore in general to add, that he left to his successor an estate highly improved, and a most respectable set of tenants, all thriving, and many of them wealthy.

Their tears, and the deep concern visible in their countenances, while in silent procession they followed him to the tomb, afforded to beholders a striking, though melancholy proof, of the place which he had held in their hearts.

To landholders in general, but particularly to proprietors of extensive estates, the Earl of Kinnoull, has furnished by his example, decided evidence, that to see with their own eyes the situation of their tenants, to hear in person their complaints, to redress them when well founded, and in all things to consult their interest, are the most infallible means of bringing real and permanent improvement to their property.

If we follow this good man into the private scenes of domestic life, his character assumes a still more amiably engaging form.

Having no children of his own body, (his only child having died an infant) his paternal affection flowed out in constant streams of tenderness to his near relations, and the numerous branches of his family. To all of them his manners were affectionate, for the sensibility of his heart was great.

In the sickness or *peculiarly distressful situation* of such of them as lived in his house, his unwearied attentions to their comfort, marked the delicacy of his mind, commanded the warmeſt returns of grateful affection from them, and excited the admiration of all who had acceſs to obſerve this part of his conduct. It is not to be wondered, therefore, that his family and immediate connexions in general, looked up to him with mingled reverence and love.

But his behaviour to his nephew the heir of his title and fortune, (the preſent Earl of Kinnoull) claims a more particular notice. Far from regarding him with that jealous eye, with which men advanced in life too often behold their ſucceſſors, the late Earl uniformly felt and expreſt for *his*, the ſtrongeſt attachment; and as the conduct of his education in early life, had been the object of his uncle's anxious attention, ſo, when grown up to manhood, he admitted him into habits of the ſtricteſt intimacy and friendship; explained to him all his plans of alteration or improvement, and the principles on which they were founded; consulted with him concerning their propriety, and the modes of carrying them into execution. Anxious, at the same time, about the future welfare of his tenants, while he introduced to them his nephew as their future master, and explained to him their various characters and circumstances, he warmly recommended to him that mild and generous plan of conduct towards them which he himself had uniformly observed. In the latter part of his life, he wished his nephew to take the entire direction of his affairs.

Conduct so truly generous and parental, obtained its natural and just reward, in the warmest filial affection and reverence upon the part of his nephew. As no person more cordially loved and valued this good man while in life, so none more unaffectedly mourned his death than he who succeeded to his rank and fortune. In the future conduct of that young Nobleman, it is hoped, that his friends and the public will discern the happy effects of those excellent principles in which he was instructed, and of that worthy example by which they were enforced.

As a *friend*, the late Earl of Kinnoull was warm and steady.——Though bred a courtier, he professed no affection which he did not feel, and though his language was glowing, it was sincere. Constant in all his attachments, even in old age he spoke of his friends with an enthusiasm which would have done credit to the generous feelings of youth. Nothing save gross misbehaviour could alienate his regards from those on whom he had bestowed them. The strictest integrity, and most delicate sense of honour, appeared in the whole of his intercourse with all to whom he stood related in any of the connexions of life.

To his servants he was a kind master, ever attentive to their comfort both in health and sickness. He felt the obligation of faithful services, and nobly rewarded them. He knew to whom confidence was due, and never indulged suspicion. And such was the general mildness and generosity of his conduct to his domestics, that to be dismissed his service was ever regarded by them as the severest punishment.

From the variety of important or interesting objects which constantly solicited and engaged his attention, it was impossible that time could hang heavy on his hands. To listlessness and languor, the common attendants of wealth and greatness, he was a stranger. His mind naturally active, and habituated to employment, was ever directed to something requiring thought or exertion; to every hour was assigned its proper employment, and in consequence of a strict and persevering arrangement, the quantity of business which he difpatched, was great. Though liberal of his money, he was a rigid œconomift of his time.

Advanced age and growing infirmities interrupted not in him the duties of the man and the Chriftian; unavoidable evils he fuftained with pious refignation, and as it pleafed God to continue with him his intellectual powers unimpaired, to the very conclufion of life, his courfe of active benevolence fcarcely fuffered an interruption. The laft acts of his life were thofe of friendfhip and charity.

From thefe imperfect fketches may be formed an idea of the character of this truly good man. To fum it up in a few words;—his piety was exalted, his benevolence large, his charity extenfive, his converfation chafte and edifying, his manners exemplary. In his whole deportment were feen, the dignity of the Nobleman, the learning of the Scholar, and the virtue of the Christian.

The approaches of death, long foreseen and familiar to his mind, he beheld with serenity and fortitude, for his confidence rested upon that foundation which he knew death itself could not shake. No words can do so much justice to his sentiments upon this subject as his own. They were exprest to the Author of the preceding Sermon, in course of a long and serious conversation upon the subject of it, a short while before his death. As the general theme was of his recommendation, so he specified some of the particular topics which he wished to be introduced in it, particularly the doctrine of the atonement.

" I have always considered the a-
" tonement of Christ," said he, " to
" be characteristical of the gospel as a
" system of religion. Strip it of that
" doctrine, and you reduce it to a scheme

" of morality, excellent indeed, and such
" as the world never saw, but to man in
" the present state of his faculties, abso-
" lutely impracticable. The atonement
" of Christ, and the truths immediately
" connected with that fundamental prin-
" ciple, provide a remedy for all the
" wants and weaknesses of our nature.
" They who strive to remove these preci-
" ous doctrines from the word of God,
" do an irreparable injury to the grand
" and beautiful system of religion which
" it contains, as well as to the comfort
" and hopes of man. *For my own part*,
" I am now an old man, and have expe-
" perienced the infirmities of advanced
" years. Of late, in the course of severe
" and dangerous illness, I have been re-
" peatedly brought to the gates of death.
" My time in this world cannot now be
" long. But with truth I can declare,
" that in midst of all my past afflictions,
" my heart was supported and comforted,

" by a firm reliance upon the merits and
" atonement of my Saviour; and now in
" the near prospect of entering upon an
" eternal world, this is the foundation,
" and the only foundation of my confi-
" dence and hope."

In thefe fentiments he fteadily perfevered till the conclufion of the fcene. His laft illnefs continued but a few days, it was a wafting and decline of nature, unattended with pain. On the 27$^{th.}$ December 1787, without a ftruggle, or groan, or change of countenance, he expired.

" MARK THE PERFECT MAN AND BE-
" HOLD THE UPRIGHT: FOR THE END OF
" THAT MAN IS PEACE."

THE PRESIDENT, DIRECTORS, AND OFFICERS,

OF THE

SOCIETY, FOR THE YEAR 1788.

EARL OF LEVEN, PRESIDENT OF THE SOCIETY.

Committee of Directors.

The EARL of HOPETON Prefident of the Committee.

Mr John Gloag Merchant in Edinburgh.

Rev. John Erſkine, D. D. Edinburgh.

Rev. William Gloag, D. D. Edinburgh.

Robert M'Intoſh, Eſq; Advocate.

Mr Iſaac Grant, Clerk to the Signet.

Mr Horatius Cannon, Clerk to the Signet.

Rev. John Kemp, Edinburgh.

Rev. Thomas Randal, Edinburgh.

Mr Andrew Hamilton.

Mr John Moncrieff.

Rev. William Paul, St. Cuthberts.

Mr Alex. Duncan, Clerk to the Signet.

John Dickſon, Eſq; Advocate.

Mr John Pitcairn, Merchant.

Officers of the Society.

Rev. John M'Farlan, D. D. Secretary.
William Galloway, Esq; Merchant in Edinburgh, Comptroller.
Robert Chalmers, Esq; Accomptant-General of Excise, Accomptant.
John Davidson, Esq; Writer to the Signet, Treasurer.
James Bonar, Clerk.
Archibald Lundie, Writer to the Signet, Bookholder.
M. Gray, front of the Exchange, Bookseller.
Mungo Watson, Beadle.

Annual and other Benefactions are received by the following Persons.

IN EDINBURGH,
By John Davidson, Esq; Writer to the Signet, Treasurer to the Society.

In London,

By Thomas Coutts, Efq; Banker in the Strand.

John M'Intofh, Efq; N° 8, North fide of the Royal Exchange, Secretary to the Society.

William Fuller, Efq; and Son, Bankers, Lombard-Street.

Form of a Bequeft or Legacy.

Item, I give and bequeath the fum of   to the Society in Scotland for Propagating Chriftian Knowledge, to be applied (to the purpofes of the firft or fecond patent, as the donor pleafes.) See both patents, p. 54 and 59, of the account of the Society, publifhed in May 1774.

Those who may be pleafed to favour this Society with Bequefts or Legacies, are intreated to express their intention in the very words above directed; and particularly to take care that the words, *in Scotland*, be not omitted.

N. B. THE uncommon length of the Sermon and Appendix, having already extended this publication to a considerable size, it was judged proper to omit the usual Annual Account of the Schools in the Society's service; but this, with other particulars respecting the Society, will soon be given to the public in a separate publication.

THE END.

www.ingramcontent.com/pod-product-compliance
Lightning Source LLC
Chambersburg PA
CBHW022132160426
43197CB00009B/1249